F. Willard Brown graduated from Cal Poly and the University of Illinois and did additional graduate work at UC Berkeley. He is an author, speaker, educator, and population activist who has worked with International Planned Parenthood, the Population Institute, and the Population Media Center. He has taught at Cal Poly, Palomar College, and UC San Diego.

F. Willard Brown

THE HUMAN MIND

AUSTIN MACAULEY PUBLISHERS™

LONDON • CAMBRIDGE • NEW YORK • SHARJAH

Ordering Information
Quantity sales: Special discounts are available on quantity purchases by corporations, associations, and others. For details, contact the publisher at the address below.

Publisher's Cataloging-in-Publication data
Brown, F. Willard
The Human Mind

ISBN 9798889105329 (Paperback)
ISBN 9798889105336 (Hardback)
ISBN 9798889105343 (ePub e-book)

Library of Congress Control Number: 2023916427

www.austinmacauley.com/us

First Published 2024
Austin Macauley Publishers LLC
40 Wall Street, 33rd Floor, Suite 3302
New York, NY 10005
USA

mail-usa@austinmacauley.com
+1 (646) 5125767

Stars, vapor, snow, the hills, rocks, the
Fifth month flowers, my amaze, my love,
Aware of the buffalo, the peace herds,
The bull, strong-breasted and hairy,
Aware of the mockingbird of
the wilds at day-break,
Solitary, singing in the West,
I strike up for a new world.

— Walt Whitman

Preface

*T*he *Human Mind* grew out of my desire to leave a book which is a compilation of the most important things I have learned in my very long life.

After a lifetime of study, I consider myself to be educated, and I am sure there are people who would disagree, and I respect their opinions. However, I say that a man who does not understand science is not fully educated, no matter what else he may know. Science is certainly the greatest achievement of the human race and I am using the word *science* in the broad sense, which includes psychology and political science. Some will say, "What about the arts?" Yes, we all enjoy and appreciate the arts, but remember that the arts have not liberated us from our ignorance. It took science to do that.

Most of the American public is scientifically illiterate, a consequence of the failure of American public education. This failure permits our leaders to get away with unscientific statements such as the denial of global warming, etc.

Yes, science has been abused, such as it was with the creation of nuclear weapons, just as any tool can be abused or misused. But this does not detract from the beauty and nobility of pure science in its pursuit of truth.

As wonderful as science is, I do not rank it in importance above self-knowledge, which is far more important than any other kind of knowing, and unfortunately for the human race, self-knowledge is sadly lacking throughout the entire world. You can see this in the transparent egotism and multiple character deficiencies of our leaders.

The chapter "Evolution and Human Consciousness" is an edited version of a lecture I gave at UCSD. In it, I have tried to show the reasons for mankind's homicidal and war-like nature. It is something every human being should understand if we are going to abandon the great evil of nationalism and have peace on this planet.

Truth

Here in the 21st century as I look out on a world of colossal ignorance and violence, what a disappointment it is that there is so little regard for truth. For most people, truth is not high on their list of priorities, if it is on the list at all. The human mind is concerned with gratification of one kind or another, such as the gratification of achievement. Truth is neglected in pursuit of various forms of comfort and gratification.

To me, if anything is sacred, it must surely be truth. There is no way untruth can be sacred. A truly religious mind is concerned only with truth; it is not mired in belief. Truth is the highest religion, and by far the most important part of truth is the truth about oneself, the truth that few want.

The scientist pursues truth relentlessly, and this accounts for the spectacular success of science. What a contrast with organized religion or politics! However, scientific truth is restricted to that which is material and that which is demonstrable. Historians are concerned with truth, if they are good historians, but of course, history, the study of the past, is not demonstrable except for the records the past has left. Obviously, our political leaders and our religious leaders have demonstrated little concern for truth.

Our human predicament requires knowledge to live intelligently. That knowledge is always limited whereas we should remember that the unknown is infinite. We try to get by with what little knowledge we have to make our way in life. Knowledge has its place, but we should bear in mind that all knowledge is limited, narrow, and binding.

When testifying in court we are asked to swear to "Tell the truth, the whole truth, and nothing but the truth." Everyone who has taken that oath has lied. What is the whole truth? The whole truth is the whole universe! Obviously, no one knows the whole truth.

On the temples of ancient Greece are the words, KNOW THYSELF. This was the supreme form of knowledge for the wisest of the ancient Greeks. But in later centuries that wisdom was forgotten. I suspect the reason the ancient Greeks accomplished so much was because of their great respect for self-knowledge. Bertrand Russell wrote, "In all history, nothing is so surprising or so difficult to account for as the sudden rise of civilization in Greece."[1] Those incredible people gave us science, mathematics, philosophy, democracy, medicine, athletics, drama, and unsurpassed arts and architecture. In other words, they gave us civilization.

Education should be life-long. Today, with the internet, we have entered the "information age." There is a superabundance of information available, along with a good deal of propaganda, and misinformation. And this is one reason education is so important: to distinguish fact from fiction.

We know that in the world today there are poor countries and rich countries. The poor countries are poor because they have a low level of education. The rich countries are rich because they are educated. It's as simple as that. I acknowledge that there are a few oil-rich countries that have a high gross domestic product per capita and a low level of education, but those exceptions are few in number. Unfortunately, many national leaders fail to give importance to educating their people. Instead, they spend large sums on armaments or palaces for themselves.

What we learn from science is that ultimately, truth is the unknown. The human mind has its limitations. For example, take the wave-particle duality of light. The mind says that light must be a wave or a particle, it can't possibly be both. But *it is both* and it is neither, because the real world does not conform to our human preconceptions.

Christians are going to ask, "If self-knowledge is so important, why did our Savior say nothing about it?" It turns out he actually did, even though you will not find one word about self-knowledge in the entire bible. But in 1898, British Archeologists in Egypt discovered a papyrus titled *The Sayings of Jesus.* You can look it up on Wikipedia. On it are the words, "The way to God is through knowing oneself." I consider this to be much more authentic than anything in the Gospels. We don't really know what Jesus said. Nothing was written down until 40 years after his death. The early Christians put words in his mouth, plus a lot of mythology, such as the virgin birth, and the various "miracles" which destroy the credibility of the account.

Those people who say they know themselves are usually the people who have not taken the first step of learning. Of course, you know the history of your life, your likes and dislikes, some of your personality traits, etc., but self-knowledge is something much deeper.

Conditioning

Most people don't even know they are conditioned. I once worked in a summer camp where I could observe other people's habits. The young men who were working there as counselors got up in the morning, shaved, and brushed their teeth because that was the way they had been conditioned. If you are going to brush your teeth once a day, the worst possible time is before your first meal. The best time is after your last meal. Immediately after every meal is best, but is not convenient for most of us. So these young men were brushing at the worst possible time, simply because that was the way their minds had been conditioned. It's a good example of how ignorance is passed on from generation to generation.

This book attempts to show the many ways that the human mind has been wrongly conditioned.

Another example of conditioning is diet. What a tragedy that we have all been brought up in ignorance of the right diet. The Standard American Diet (SAD) kills twice as many Americans every year as Covid 19. Yet almost no one is saying anything about it. Food addiction is a psychological problem. Instead of being addicted to animal products and junk food, we could be conditioned to a scientific diet, which, incidentally, can be just as delicious as the SAD. For further information on diet, see Chapter 9.

In one study in the U.K., a group was told about the correct, optimum, diet and were given all the facts. In the end, only 30% adopted the correct diet. That is a good illustration of the power of food addiction.

One of the worst addictions is sugar. Food companies put sugar in everything to make their products addictive. There is a website everyone should see called "146 WAYS THAT SUGAR IS RUINING YOUR HEALTH." It lists 146 peer-reviewed scientific papers showing some of the bad effects of sugar in our diets. It has also been scientifically established that sugar causes brain damage. Children should never be permitted to eat candy or any kind of sweets.

You can test for sugar addiction in yourself by avoiding anything that contains sugar for a week. If you then have a craving for something sweet, it means you test positive.

Jesus is quoted as having said, "If any man come to me, and hate not his father and mother, and wife, and children, and brethren, and sisters, yea, and his own life also, he cannot be my disciple." Luke 14:26, (KJV). That is a bit of scripture you will never hear in church. And I think that it is one of the things that Jesus actually did say. What he is saying there is that we must be free of our conditioning. Of course, that word *conditioning* was unknown in his day. And the conditioning influences were mostly family and friends in that era, plus organized religion. There was no media. The printing press was not invented for another 1600 years.

Socrates said, "An unexamined life is not worth living." And most lives are unexamined.

14

Free Will

To Bertrand Russell's list of "Ideas That Have Harmed Mankind"[i] I would like to add the idea of free will. This concept is a complete illusion and has been enormously harmful to mankind.

Of course, I am free to buy that car or not buy that car, but my choice will be entirely determined by the content of my consciousness. The human mind is a programmed computer and what I do or think is the result of that programming. That programming is the sum total of what has been recorded in my mind in the past; both the genetic past and the environmental past. So there is no free will, only cause and effect. And since there is no free will, there is no sin. What is called sin is always the result of ignorance. This is one reason why self-knowledge is so important. The mind is conditioned by the morality of the world, which is really immorality. The entire justice system is predicated on the illusion of free will. The concept permeates all of our thinking.

The reader may ask, what about greed, hate, and lust, aren't they the cause of sin? But greed, hate, and lust are entirely the result of self-ignorance, which is the worst kind of ignorance.

Winston Churchill wrote, "The human mind, except when guided by extraordinary genius, cannot surmount the established conclusions amid which it has been reared." I think "extraordinary genius" might be an overstatement, except for the conditioning we get before the age of 12. The point is we are all conditioned, by our parents, by our friends, by our teachers, by the media, etc. A conditioned mind cannot be free, and there must be freedom for there to be intelligence.

J. Krishnamurti[ii] asks, "If there is will, is there freedom?" To find out what freedom really is, I refer you to his *Commentaries on Living*, the most significant book ever written. Unfortunately, Krishnamurti is a Hindu name, which immediately creates prejudice. But Krishnamurti is not a Hindu, his teaching has nothing to do with Eastern religion or philosophy. Krishnamurti is for people who want reality, and most people do not want reality.

What is will? Obviously, it is the desire that leads to action. And desire is a conflict in consciousness between what I have and what I do not have. And so will is conflict.

It is possible to live without any conflict of any kind. This requires constant awareness and observation of conflict as it arises.

Evolution and Human Consciousness

Our human race is the result of a million years of evolution and an understanding of mankind is impossible without an understanding of how the human race has evolved.

The word evolution means a gradual and progressive change, whether it be applied to galaxies, stars, geology, human culture, or biology. It has been said that it is impossible to understand God without understanding evolution because evolution is a fundamental part of creation. In any event, the world we now have is the result of billions of years of evolution.

With regard to biology, contrary to popular belief, there is no such thing as the *theory* of evolution. Biological evolution is not a theory but an established scientific fact and there is no controversy about this amongst biologists. There are different theories (that's plural, not singular) to explain evolution, but evolution itself is a scientific fact. These different theories do not conflict with each other but are mutually complimentary and supportive.

I notice that recently even the Catholic Church, after opposing Darwinism for a century, has come to acknowledge the fact of evolution, and I would think this could create enormous doctrinal problems for them. Actually, biological evolution is an old idea, going back to ancient Greece. The Greeks had a lot of ideas, so it is not surprising that some of them turned out to be right.

But no one explained how one life form could evolve into another until 1809 when a Frenchman named Jean-Baptiste Lamarck provided a mechanism by which organic evolution could take place.

His hypothesis very neatly explained many things, but there was one trouble: it happened to be wrong. Lamarck's hypothesis depended on the inheritance of acquired characteristics which we now know does not happen.

The big name in evolution, of course, is Charles Darwin, who was born on the same day in 1809 as Abraham Lincoln. I suppose astrologers could make something of that fact, and perhaps there is a parallel: Lincoln freed the slaves and Darwin freed the world of its ignorance, at least our ignorance about evolution.

Darwin's momentous book was titled *On the Origin of Species* and was first published in 1859. This was one of the greatest scientific breakthroughs in history, and in biology, I would say *the* greatest breakthrough, even including the recent breaking of the genetic code.

The elements of Darwinism are as follows:

(1) **Heredity:** Darwin knew that characteristics tend to be inherited but he did not know the laws of genetics. These laws were not discovered until 1865 by Gregor Mendel. And because Mendel published his discovery in an obscure journal, his

findings were ignored until 1900 when they were rediscovered.

(2) **Variation**: This simply means that two individuals of the same species are never exactly alike except in the case of identical twins. There is always variation. Any characteristic that you can measure, whether it be blood pressure in alligators or the length of puppy tails, it will follow the classic bell-shaped probability distribution, where the farther away you move from the average, the less likely that value will occur.

(3) **Excess Replication:** Every species of plant or animal will reproduce excessively, and only a small percentage of offspring will live to pass on their genes to the next generation. The others must perish. Darwin was familiar with the work of Thomas Malthus who pointed out that an unchecked population will grow geometrically. Geometric growth is what we now call exponential. For instance, if the population doubles every generation, in only 20 generations a mating pair can have a million descendants. This does not happen in nature because of natural checks such as predators. Mankind has learned to defeat these natural checks, and this is why the world is so overpopulated with our species. We have death control, which everyone agrees is a good thing, but it is not balanced with birth control. I think the worst consequence of overpopulation is the large and irreversible environmental damage to the planet.

(4) **Natural Selection:** I would say that unless you understand natural selection you are not an educated person, no matter what else you know. Because of excess replication, most plants and animals are doomed to perish without producing progeny. And there is a difference between the individuals that survive and those that do not survive. The ones that survive may just be lucky, but the probability is that they are more fit for survival in some way. And that's natural selection: nature is constantly weeding out those individuals who are less fit for survival. A classic example is the giraffe: why is it so tall? Tallness is an obvious advantage in reaching leaves higher up on a tree. And so, over many generations the taller animals had a better chance to survive and were therefore selected by nature to pass on their tallness genes to future generations, resulting in the tall giraffe we know today.

So, you can see that given the above four elements, evolution must inevitably occur because nature is constantly doing exactly what breeders do when they selectively breed a desired characteristic into a plant or animal. As Thomas Huxley said, "How extremely stupid not to have thought of it." Like many great ideas, it seems almost obvious after someone points it out. But it's worth noting that it took 3,000 years of civilization before someone did point it out.

Darwin's work is sometimes called the Darwinian Revolution because it revolutionized human thinking more than any other scientific discovery. Understanding Darwinism gives you an understanding of nature and also an understanding of man who is a part of nature.

Darwin also contributed to the idea of sexual selection. This was introduced in *On the Origin of Species* and amplified in a later book, *The Descent of Man, and Selection in Relation to Sex*, published in 1871.

Sexual selection is an important evolutionary concept because it explains so many things that cannot be explained with natural selection. Here, the selecting element is success in mating. Obviously, mere survival does not ensure that your genes are going to be transmitted to the next generation. You must also be successful at mating. Sexual selection explains such phenomena as the peacock's tail, which certainly has no survival value, but it is important for attracting a peahen. And so, over many generations, peacocks with the more attractive tails were more successful at mating, and peacock tails became more and more elaborate. It's worth noting that in bird species where the female does the selecting, it is the male that is colorful, whereas in the human species where the male has done the selecting (this may not be true currently), it is the female that is the "fair sex."

Another example of sexual selection in humans is skin color. People come in different colors. The human race originated in Africa and I'm sure that at the beginning everyone was about the same color which was probably quite dark. But now we have fair-skinned people who are deficient in melanin. There is no survival value to the loss of this pigmentation. In fact, quite the opposite, fair-skinned people are susceptible to ultra-violet skin damage which causes sunburn and skin cancer. In Europe especially, people have fair skins because of sexual selection which has discriminated against darker skins over the millennia. (This analysis agrees with Darwin's view but is contrary to the current convention. However, I believe that Darwin and not current thinking is correct for reasons that I will not go into here.)

Much has been added to organic evolution since Darwin's day, such as the importance of mutations. These have a number of causes; one such is nuclear radiation. Mutations can produce sudden changes in only one generation. Of course, 99 percent of mutations are unfavorable, but every ten thousand years or so a mutation will occur which is beneficial, and the mutant will have a better chance of survival and pass on the favorable change to its offspring.

Evolution through mutation can explain changes that cannot be explained through variation such as the transition from a three-chambered heart to a four-chambered heart. The four-chambered heart evolved independently in both birds and mammals. This is called parallel evolution.

As I indicated, Darwin did not hesitate to apply his ideas to the descent of man. The human species had already been placed in the primate family 50 years before Darwin was even born. Darwin, along with other naturalists, concluded from the anatomical evidence that the apes and man have had a common ancestry. Naturally, this created problems for those people who wanted to believe in the biblical account of creation. Even today there are people, known as creationists, who oppose the whole idea of evolution. These people have a problem with the steady progression of life from the simplest lifeform to man. For instance, imagine a timeline like this:

***

At the left end of this line, you have the simplest form of life which is little more than a complicated molecule. Then there is a steady progression in complexity along this evolutionary line until you come to the more advanced forms of life at the right end, and to the man who regards himself as the highest form of life and who has assigned to himself an immortal soul. So then, the theological question arises, at what point on this line of gradual change does this soul appear? Of course, you can pick some point and say this is it; but that raises another question of why that point and not some other.

And so, evolution has dethroned man from the high pedestal on which he had placed himself.

Unfortunately, the creationists have been quite successful at times in imposing their ignorance on our children. For instance, in Alabama, textbooks are pasted with warnings saying that evolution is a controversial theory, not a fact. The creationists have a psychological problem, resulting from a conflict between belief and actuality.

Man is a unique species in three significant ways:

(1)   Man is the only species in the homo genus.

(2)   Man is the only species that engages in premeditated warfare.

(3)   Man possesses a brain much larger than is needed for survival.

I suspect these three facts are not unrelated, and in fact, the third one is the consequence of the other two. Warfare has been going on for a long time and is still going on. It has played an important part in the evolution of homo sapiens.

Obviously, defeated people are not going to pass on their genes to future generations, as the victors do. And it's not the more peaceful tribes who come out on top. The more ruthless and violent side is often the winning side. Mental cunning is going to render an advantage in any war, both for strategy and for the invention of superior weapons.

So you can see that natural selection is going to favor the tribes with superior intelligence. This has been going on for probably at least a million years.

There is only one species now in the human genus. It wasn't always that way. In the past, there were other species such as Homo Neanderthalensis. What happened to the other species? The most likely answer is that they were done in by our murderous ancestors. Louis Leakey was struck by the number of early Hominid skulls he found that had holes in them. He attributes the holes to homicide and warfare.

We are the product of all those hundreds of millennia of violence. As a result, there is in man a powerful homicidal instinct. Most of us at one time or another, have experienced the urge to kill. Now you know where that urge comes from. In civilized people, this instinct is usually sublimated into something mild like character assassination. That word *assassination* is the right word; it is a psychological murder.

And warfare in civilized societies is reduced to battles on the playing field, in what is called sports.

Genocide is not something new; the word is new, but not the practice. You can see the psychological residue of genocide in modern man in issues like racism and xenophobia.

The mind of man, you see, is millions of years old the day we are born. This is something the psychologists have only recently found out. They could have found it out long ago through meditation. But, like most people, psychologists do not meditate.

I am reluctant to use that word because there are now all kinds of nonsense called meditation which is not meditation at all. For instance, 30 years ago there was a form of mantra yoga that was popular. It was called Transcendental Meditation. Trouble is, it's not transcendental and it's not meditation. True meditation means deep awareness of your own consciousness, without any judgment of any kind.

Meditation leads to self-knowledge which is far more important than any other kind of knowledge and it is also the last thing on earth that most people want. This is the tragedy of the human race: the most important thing in life is also the last thing anyone wants to know. The great Chinese philosopher Lao Tse said, "The sage is concerned with the inner and not with the outer world."

Today no one tells you to know yourself.[iii] You are told to control yourself, but the problem is that the controller is the controlled, and the controller has been conditioned by the insanity and immorality of the world.

I think the reason Sigmund Freud had such great insights was that he was one of the few people in history who looked at his own consciousness. Much to his credit. But if you study Freud, you learn about Freud, not about yourself.

Benjamin Franklin said, "There are three things extremely hard: steel, diamond, and to know oneself."

The only things you get from self-knowledge are sanity, maturity, and wisdom. There is no gratification to it.

And that is one reason why so few people pursue it. However, if we are really earnest about learning about ourselves, we will learn. We can learn from pure observation of every thought through choiceless awareness.

Malthus Revisited

mongst economists, it is currently fashionable to downgrade Thomas Malthus, so it's important to understand just where Malthus was right and where he went wrong.

Malthus pointed out that populations grow exponentially. He used the word "geometrically" as in geometric progression, but in modern usage, we would say exponentially. And he was certainly right; the population of any species will grow exponentially if there are no checks. Normally there are no enduring population explosions in wild species because nature provides checks. Unfortunately, there is one species that has learned to defeat all the checks and that, of course, is the human species.

Malthus also predicted that eventually, England would not be able to feed herself. He was right about that, also. England has not been able to feed herself for more than one hundred years. The country endures on imported food. This works well for England, but if every country tries to be a food-importing country, it doesn't take much imagination to see there are going to be problems.

Today the world is so overpopulated that 45,000 people die every day from starvation and malnutrition. But even with those deaths, global population is still increasing by 220,000 more people every day.

Some claim that technology is going to save us. As a technologist, I can assure you that not every problem is amendable to a technological solution.

And there are those who claim that an increase in population will give us more geniuses who will then save us. I think it is reasonable to assume that perhaps one person in a million could be called a super-genius. That means we have 8,000 of these people in the global population. So, where are those people? Why aren't they saving us? The geniuses I know all say the same thing: our planet is being destroyed.

We think we are superior to other species, but the human species is the only species that pollutes. And now we have soil pollution, water pollution, and air pollution levels which threaten all forms of life on our planet. 30,000 species are being destroyed every year. It is the greatest mass extinction in the last 65 million years.

Few people realize the power of exponential growth. Gabor Zovanyi has pointed out that if our species had started with just two people 10,000 years ago and then increased at a rate of only one percent per year, today humanity would be a solid ball of flesh many light years in diameter. I thought this must be in error until I did the math. For the last 200 years, the population has grown by not one percent, but by 2.2 percent. Stephen Hawking calculated that if this continues with the population doubling every 40 years, by the year 2600 there will be standing room only on our planet.

What is also seldom realized is that another consequence of a high birth rate is social instability as manifested by terrorism, insurgencies, violent demonstrations, and rebellions. This is amply explained and documented in *The Security Demographic: Population and Civil Conflict after the Cold War* by Richard P. Cincotta, et al. You may have noticed that socially unstable countries almost always have a high birthrate.

Today our planet is horribly overpopulated. The sustainable population has been calculated to be 2 billion. We now have 8 billion and another 81 million is added every year. By sustainable we mean a world where everyone can enjoy a European lifestyle.

That is where everyone can have a furnished apartment with hot and cold running water, a refrigerator, a computer, and a small car, or at least a bicycle. People from poor countries now risk their lives to attain that standard of living by attempting to immigrate to Europe or North America.

One encouraging sign is that the most advanced countries have achieved a negative population growth rate. That is something they should be proud of. Instead, some of those governments are troubled about a population decline and have actually taken measures to increase the birth rate! That illustrates the great evil of nationalism. Let us remember, if there was no nationalism, there would be no wars. But the immaturity of nationalism prevails in every country.

And there seems to be some kind of strange taboo against ever mentioning overpopulation as the root cause of this planet's enormous environmental problems. The planet is being destroyed by excessive human numbers.

Belief

It has been going on for thousands of years, perhaps a million. It occurs throughout the entire world: in the Arctic, the Eskimo has his beliefs, and in Africa, the Pygmy has his beliefs. Something as universal as belief doesn't just happen—there are powerful psychological forces that cause belief. Understanding those forces are part of self-knowledge, the knowledge that no one wants. But without self-knowledge, sanity is not possible. The primary compulsion for belief is fear. The man who is free of fear has no need for any belief about anything.

Obviously, most people have beliefs, religious beliefs, political beliefs, superstitious beliefs, etc. And belief causes division, between one man and another; hundreds of wars have been fought because of belief. For scores of decades, wars were fought between Protestants and Catholics, both sides calling themselves Christians. Obviously, nothing could be more un-Christian than warfare.

Do we need belief? If I believe the earth is flat, I am not going to learn about the shape of the earth, because I already know that the earth is flat, and that is the end of it. And so belief fosters a closed mind as well as ignorance and division. Like knowledge, belief is narrow and limited; if you have belief, you can't have truth. Remember that Truth is the unknown. Belief is always of the known. It may be obvious to us that the belief of the Islamist is false, it is not so easy to see that our own beliefs are also false.

The human mind seeks security and there is psychological satisfaction in having an explanation for the mysteries of life and the universe, even when that explanation is wrong.

You will notice that what people believe is usually gratifying or comforting in some way, such as life after death, the fantasy of heaven and hell, and reincarnation. Of course, eternal damnation is not appealing, but that is something we want for our enemies, not for ourselves. Justice is a human invention; there is certainly no justice in nature. We want the wicked to be punished and the righteous to be rewarded, and since real life often provides the opposite, we have invented divine justice which must take place after death.

Gandhi said, "All religions are true." That was the politically correct thing to say, but if he had been honest, he would have said all religions are false. All religions certainly have failed to bring peace in the world; instead, they have caused strife and wars.

Obviously, a mind that is seeking comfort is not concerned with truth. Truth is liberating but generally not comforting; and why should it be?

Mankind has been inventing images of God for thousands of years. Some of those images are naive, some are more sophisticated, but all are wrong.

I ask my students, "What is infinity minus one?" Most know that it is still infinity. And it doesn't matter if you subtract ten to the power of one hundred, which, incidentally, is an inconceivably large number. So what does this say? (It says, doesn't it?) that *there is no relation between the finite and the infinite.*

It is important to understand that we humans are finite beings, limited in time and space. Limited in time because we are mortal. Limited in space, because unless we are astronauts, we are confined to spend our lives on or near the surface of this one planet. And the powers of the mind are very limited.

So here is this finite entity trying to reach out and grasp the infinite! How absurd! And that is why all attempts to prove or disprove the existence of God will fail. They always have.

As long ago as the 14th century, the great theologian Meister Eckhart wrote, "Why prate you of God? Whatever you say of God is untrue." He was right. And, not surprisingly, he got in trouble for saying such things.

There is no relation between the finite and the infinite.

A truly religious mind will be concerned only with truth, it will have no beliefs about anything.

Sanity

It should not be confused with normalcy. The norm is the average and the average person suffers from depression, which has been called, "the common cold of mental illness." The average mind also has numerous neurotic conflicts.

Sanity is rare but it is possible. It requires self-knowledge, which is gained through meditation. Again, most of what is called meditation is not meditation at all. True meditation means observation of what the mind is doing from moment to moment. Meditation is not something separate from everyday life. It must be an ongoing process. It means choiceless awareness without any goal of self-improvement or "getting somewhere". It is only the ego that wants to "get somewhere" and we can't be sane if we have an ego. The human ego is responsible for all the violence and greed of mankind. It has been said that a man is mature to the degree that he knows himself.[3]

Few people know themselves deeply. And those people who say, "Oh, of course, I know myself," are usually the people who have not taken the first step of looking at their own consciousness.

Sanity means being free of all conflict. That requires constant awareness of conflict as it arises. Conflict always arises from the self; when there is no self, there is no conflict. Of course, anger is conflict, frustration is conflict, but the pursuit of an ideal is also conflict.

It has also been said, "Self-perfection is the denial of virtue."[3] True virtue comes from love, not from ambition. Love is a terribly abused word. Despite all the propaganda to the contrary, love is not desire, it is not possession. Love is not thought, love is always pure. Thought is always conditioned by the past, and the past is certainly not pure. And love is factual, not emotional. [3]

If you are honest, you will admit that what is important to you in life is yourself. And so what is this self to which our minds have given such enormous importance? This is an immense question, and it is the question that matters, not the answer. Anyone can answer the question, but it is the question that matters; we need to stay with the question. Any answer is a conclusion, and the word *conclusion* means an ending. An ending of all inquiry and discovery, an ending of all learning, an ending of openness. Obviously, the self is a concept, a conclusion, a deeply rooted habit of thought, but does it have any reality beyond that? It is important to understand that the self has been created by the mind and is illusory. The mind is not you.

The mind has concluded that it is separate from the universe, from creation. But, in fact, there is only the universe, only creation that exists; we are part of it. The conclusion that we are separate from creation has been called the universal delusion of mankind. This delusion becomes apparent when you consider phrases like, "I've made up my mind." As if there is a "me" who possesses a mind!

Thought is present every waking hour and thought has created a thinker. But is there really a thinker, or is there only thought?

If we look at thought we will find that thought always has a motive, and the motive is desire or fear. Both desire and fear are two sides of the same coin. You don't have one without the other. Obviously, fear is self-concern. So there will be fear as long as there is a self.

The self is also an image, which is another reason why it is false. All images that the mind creates are false because they are based on experience, and experience is always limited. The image is never real. We form images of our family members, our friends, celebrities, etc., and then we relate to those images, not to the real person, who is quite different from the image the mind has created.

The self can come to an end, but there is no action of the self that will end it. It only ends through self-knowledge. All thought is conditioned by the past. If the past had been different, the mind would be different. So, knowing this, where is that autonomous self, with its free will?

Breeding

Parenthood is an immense responsibility; every parent must be a combination of doctor, nutritionist, psychologist, educator and sociologist. The average parent is a failure at parenting. And you may have noticed that it is usually the ignorant that do the most breeding. Ignorance is passed on from generation to generation, just as useful knowledge is. As parents, we make the same mistakes that our own parents made.

In these days of massive overpopulation, you are certainly not helping the planet by breeding. Furthermore, there is the genetic factor; people with bad genes, and most of us have bad genes, should not pass those bad genes on to future generations. Unfortunately, most couples do not even consider genetics when reproducing.

There is also the financial factor. By the time your child is 18 years old, you will have spent a minimum of $300,000 on the child. That's *without* counting college. This sum is the minimum; obviously, there is no maximum. That figure is something every high school graduate should know. The important things in life are not taught in school.

Furthermore, there is a five percent chance your child will be born with a serious birth defect, no matter who you are. You could be burdened with their care for the rest of your life.

Aspiring parents should consider adoption. When you adopt, you are not contributing to the population crisis. There is a super-abundance of un-adopted orphans around the world that you can choose from. Some couples may say, "But we want one of our own." They don't seem to understand that an adopted child *will be* their own. We are all part of the same human family; we are all the same species, even the separate races. An adopted child is not an extraterrestrial alien.

The pope has tried to make birth control a sin. Of course, he wants more Catholics, but is this an honorable way to get more Catholics, by condemning millions of indigent women around the world to lives of misery and poverty? The Church is not even consistent about this belief: in the Middle Ages, for example, there was a pope who actually *encouraged* birth control.

All children deserve two good parents. All the statistics on unemployment, mental illness, suicide, crime, alcoholism, divorce, etc. show that single-parent families are dysfunctional; they don't work. And every child deserves and needs love.

In the United States, there is a great deal of division about abortion. No one likes abortion, every abortion is a tragedy, but so is an unwanted child. Every child should be precious! If people would behave themselves there would be no need for abortion as a birth-control measure. But people do not behave themselves, and in view of overpopulation, and widespread poverty and homelessness, we should accept Roe vs. Wade.

Diet

For the first time in human history, we now know what we should eat and what we should not eat. What we should not eat is what most of us are eating: the Standard American Diet. The SAD is what killed my father, he was an MD, and like most MDs, he knew nothing about diet or nutrition. The SAD kills millions of Americans every year. The Center for Disease Control says that eggs alone kill 100,000 Americans annually.

The optimum, correct diet is a vegan diet. This is science, not opinion. Primates have a vegetarian intestinal tract, and homo sapiens is the only primate that is not a vegetarian.

There is a very important book on diet written by Dr. Michael Greger: *How Not to Die.*[1] Be sure to read the preface and introduction. You will be appalled by what you learn about the medical industry, the pharmaceutical industry, and the food industry. Dr. Greger backs up everything he says with more than 2,000 references to scientific literature. It's all science, not opinion. There are also some excellent videos available on YouTube by Dr. Joel Fuhrman, and be sure to see, "What the Dairy Industry Doesn't Want You to Know" by Dr. Neal Barnard.

The cause-and-effect relationship between diet and health is much stronger and more pervasive than is realized by either the general public or the medical profession. This is a giant gap left in the training of our doctors.

I was in the hospital recently and ordered Vegan meals. They were provided, and were delicious, but were loaded with sugar and artificial preservatives. So even the hospitals are serving junk food!

The human race has learned to make dishes that are delicious, but we should remember that there is no relation between what tastes good and what is nutritionally good. A scientific diet can be just as delicious as a junk-food diet. We need to educate our doctors. I have educated my doctor; she is now a Vegan and her husband is a Vegan.

To educate your doctor, direct him to the excellent videos on YouTube by Dr. Joel Fuhrman. If your primary care doctor is a good doctor, he will ask you what you had for breakfast, what you had for lunch, etc.

In the United States, every kind of animal product is now available in vegan form. You can reform your diet without even changing your menu! My wife even found vegan sour cream and vegan yogurt. You may have to go to a specialty food store or large supermarket to find everything.

Usually the best produce is raw produce. But Dr. Greger says that the anti-oxidant powers of celery are actually enhanced by cooking. I always eat the broccoli florets raw but cook the stems after chopping them up. I add some mustard powder, also on Dr. Greger's advice.

There are 5 reasons why everyone should be a vegan:

(1)   **Health and Longevity.** Many people who have suffered chronic health problems for years find that their problems miraculously disappear after switching to a scientific diet. Of course, you can have a bad vegan diet. If your vegan diet consists of French fries and Oreos, you will experience no benefit whatever. Avoid processed foods. The correct diet maximizes raw fruits and vegetables. Dr. Fuhrman says to remember GT BOMBS. G for greens, T for tomatoes, B for beans, O for onions, M for mushrooms, B for berries, and S for seeds, which includes nuts, of course.

In 1986, the famous gynecologist, Malcolm Potts, told me that the age of menarche was declining in the United States. He did not know the reason at the time. We now know the cause: farmers had been giving their livestock growth hormone so their animals would grow faster and they could make more money. The FDA should not permit that practice. Every girl is entitled to a normal childhood. All animal products, including dairy, are carcinogenic. And your chances of avoiding Alzheimer's or Parkinson's disease are greatly improved with a vegan diet.

(2)   **Global Warming.** The vast herds of livestock around the world generate more greenhouse gases than even motor vehicles. We could get away with a carnivorous diet in 1930 when the world's population was only 2 billion, but now

it is 8 billion and we simply can no longer get away with it.

(3)   **Inefficiency.** It takes eight times as much land area raising cattle compared to raising the same amount of food as plants. This is an important consideration in today's overpopulated world where 45,000 people die every day from starvation and malnutrition. If everyone was vegan, we could return vast tracts of land back to nature and save endangered species.

(4)   **Animal Rights.** When you buy meat, you are killing an animal. When you pay someone else to do the killing, it is morally the same as doing it yourself. People spend billions on their dogs and cats but commit mass murder on other mammalian species. Maybe you can see the contradiction in this, or maybe it is invisible. There are people who say they love animals but then they eat meat. Murdering animals for food is both immoral and barbaric. Many people can't understand that, because of their parental conditioning. We get our morality from our parents and so barbarism is passed on from generation to generation.

(5)   **Monoculture.** "Many of humanity's most loathed infections originated from animals." When you have a large number of the same species concentrated in a small area, any disease affecting one animal can quickly spread throughout the herd. This is how swine flu and bird flu started and spread to humans. There are

many other examples where a virus gets established in farm animals and then is transferred to humans.

Science has shown that meat in any amount is harmful. It's tragic that the human race has lived so long in ignorance. We would not have to spend all those billions and trillions on health care if people would live intelligently. And we would not have to die in our sixties, seventies or eighties.

Of course, most people are food addicts. And the food industry does everything possible to promote food addiction by loading their products with sugar, salt, and fat. Americans eat way too much of all three. Sugar is particularly destructive to health. See the article, "146 Reasons Why Sugar Ruins Your Health" at HammerNutrition.com. We now know that sugar causes brain damage. Children should not be permitted to eat candy or anything that contains sugar. The reason two-thirds of Americans are overweight is probably because two-thirds are sugar addicted. Sugar addiction is like alcoholism; both of these addictions affect the brain in a way that makes it hard to stop. You can test for sugar addiction easily by eating nothing with sugar in it for a week. If you have a craving for something sweet, it means you test positive. Of course, it is the refined sugar that is harmful; the sugar in fruit is beneficial and completely harmless. And harmless sweeteners such as Stevia are now available that can be substituted for sugar in all applications.

Living intelligently means a vegan diet, no tobacco, no narcotics, no alcohol, no junk food, and adequate exercise.

The medical industry is finally beginning to learn the importance of diet. They use the phrase "plant-based" because they don't want to use the word "vegan," which is the word they should use. Many processed foods are beginning to use "plant-based" on their labels.

The only possible deficiency in a Vegan diet is vitamin B12. You will normally not get enough of this essential vitamin unless you take a B12 supplement or use nutritional yeast. The latter is preferable because B12 supplements are not vegan. And natural yeast has a nice cheesy flavor which tastes good on a salad.

Every day you see on the streets victims of the SAD, the kind of people who take up two seats on the bus. It wasn't like that in the old days, before there was so much processed food and so much addictive junk food.

Dr. Greger has a valuable website: nutritionfacts.org. It provides an encyclopedia of facts about nutrition and health. You can also sign up for his free news service which gives you the latest research findings every day.

Alcohol in any form is harmful to health. That includes beer and wine. If you think red wine is beneficial, remember you can get the same benefit from grape juice. Alcoholism is a disease and the way to avoid that disease is to be a teetotaler. Never be ashamed to say that you don't imbibe. Set a good example for your friends. For social drinking, just ask for fruit juice.

Fasting

Juice fasting is wonderful. Everyone should fast, especially those who are overweight. I recommend a 5-day juice fast to detoxify. It's the only thing that makes me feel 40 years younger. Hunger is not a problem; if there is any hunger, you just drink fruit juice and the hunger disappears. I use plain old orange juice. Be sure your juice is 100% pure. There are many products in the supermarket doctored up with high fructose corn syrup and other additives. Thanks to the Food and Drug Administration, these imitation juices cannot use the word "juice." They are instead called "cocktail," "punch," "drink," "nectar," or some other name. Always read the ingredients on anything you consume! Avoid all products that contain sugar or preservatives.

Fasting will get your weight down faster than dieting, and you also get enormous health benefits. If you do a prolonged fast, you will need to take multivitamins to avoid a vitamin deficiency. See *The Juice Fasting Bible* by Sandra Cabot, MD (Ulysses Press, 2007). Dr. Greger, (nutritionfacts.org), has ten videos on fasting.

It's unfortunate that so many people are too cowardly to even try fasting because their fear prevents them from learning about the wonderful health benefits.

I don't know who started this idea of 3 meals a day, but I regard it as a bad idea. The average American eats about twice as much as is needed. With 2 meals a day, your stomach has time to recover for up to 12 hours between meals. I eat at 5 AM and 5 PM.

If anyone is interested, this is what I eat. I make no claim that it is optimum or that a nutritionist would approve, but it is entirely Vegan and it seems to serve me well. Breakfast is muesli made from quick oats, raisins, 3 chopped dates, unsweetened almond milk, a few sunflower seeds, chopped fruit, which is usually apple in winter, and nectarines in summer, and flaxseed meal for Omega 3. In addition, unsweetened apple sauce mixed with raw peanuts. I heat the mueslis warm, but not cooked.

Breakfast is a sweet meal and supper is a savory meal consisting of a big vegetable salad. I try to include everything in Dr. Fuhrman's GT BOMBS (See page 39). I heat the salad in the microwave so that it is warm, but not cooked. Dr. Greger says we should eat our vegetables with fat, so for that, I use peanut butter, usually spread on a Tostada. The Tostada is my only concession to Junk food. All processed foods should be avoided.

Intelligence

Most psychologists think human intelligence is something that can be measured. The first measurements were made by a Frenchman named Alfred Binet in about 1905. Binet worked with children and he pioneered the concept of mental age (MA) and intelligence quotient. The mental age of a child is simply the chronological age (CA) of an average child who scores the same on an intelligence test. So if we have a 5-year-old who scores as high as an average 6-year-old, the child would have a mental age of 6 years and his intelligence quotient would be 6 divided by 5, or 1.2. For IQ, this would be multiplied by 100 to give an IQ of 120. So IQ is always MA/CA times 100.

Like almost everything in biology, IQ follows a normal distribution curve, sometimes called the bell curve. It is also called a Gaussian distribution after Carl Friedrich Gauss, the German mathematician who worked out the equation of this curve. The mean IQ of 100 is in the center and most people lie close to the mean. In fact, 95% of the population is between 70 and 130. Below 70 are people we call retarded and those people above 130 we call gifted. Unfortunately, the curve gets closer and closer to zero the higher you go in IQ. So when you get way up to 200, the Newtons and Einsteins are very rare indeed.

If you plot mental age against chronological age, you get a straight line. If it is an average person with an IQ of 100, the slope will be 1.00. IQ is the slope of the line times 100. Unfortunately, the line does not keep going up throughout our lifetime, and in fact, it stops going up at the age of 15. So the average adult has a mental age of 15 years. Now of course with age knowledge and maturity increase, but this has nothing to do with native intelligence, which is the concept of IQ.

One criticism of IQ is the idea that the curve flattens out at the same age for everyone, while everything else in nature varies. For instance, you could have a below-average IQ but if the individual matures late, you would end up with an above-average adult. Very late maturity is what distinguishes the human species from the other primates. So if your teenager seems hopelessly immature, take heart, there are benefits to late maturity. In this regard, I should mention that the highest IQ ever recorded was made by a chimpanzee because these animals mature very early compared to human primates, and one specimen was able to score as high as a 2 ½-year-old human when it was only one year old.

Another criticism of IQ is that it improves slightly with education, which should not happen if it truly measures only native or genetic intelligence. And there are some who say the only thing an IQ test measures is your ability to score on an IQ test.

And so the concept of IQ is not a complete success. But neither is it a complete failure. It has good predictive value for academic achievement, for instance.

In 1983 a psychologist named Howard Gardener rejected the whole concept of IQ. He has introduced the concept of multiple intelligences, and gives a list of seven which are as follows:

(1) Kinematic
(2) Mathematical
(3) Musical
(4) Verbal
(5) Spatial
(6) Interpersonal
(7) Intrapersonal

Since 1983 he has added a couple more to this list. He thinks this is a much more realistic way to view intelligence because a given individual could be a musical genius and at the same time a mathematical moron. Or, vice-versa.

Kinematic intelligence is the type needed by professional athletes. Mathematical and Musical are fairly obvious. IQ test measure mostly spatial and verbal and logical. A high level of verbal intelligence is needed by writers and lawyers. A high level of spatial intelligence is needed by engineers and mechanics. Interpersonal intelligence is the type needed by politicians, executives, and salesmen.

Now we come to *intrapersonal* intelligence, which in my view is more important than all the others put together – because this type of intelligence will determine your degree of success in life and your mental health. And by success I do not mean making money. Just as interpersonal intelligence is needed to understand other people; *intrapersonal* intelligence is needed to understand yourself. People with low levels of intrapersonal intelligence tend to be alcoholics, ne'er-do-wells, and criminals, even though they may be gifted in other areas. Ted Kazinsky, for instance, is an example of a mathematical genius with a low level of intrapersonal intelligence. Another example is Edgar Allen Poe, who obviously had a high level of verbal intelligence, but he was an alcoholic.

Not surprisingly, the experts have trouble agreeing on a definition of intelligence. One of my encyclopedias defines it as "A general capacity of an individual to adjust his thinking to new requirements." My other encyclopedia gives a somewhat similar definition; it says intelligence is "The ability to make use of past experience in adjusting to new situations."

But the definition I like best comes from my mentor,[3] who gets it down to one word. He says, "Intelligence is understanding."

Endnotes

[i] Bertrand Russel, A History of Western Philosophy (Simon and Schuster, 1945).

[ii] J. Krishnamurti, Commentaries on Living, Volumes 1, 2, and 3 (Quest Books, 1956).

[iii] Having said that, I have found two exceptions. One is Berliner and McLarney, Management Practice and Training, page 542, Richard D. Irwin, Inc., 1974. The other is Koontz and O'Donnell, Essentials of Management, page 348, McGraw Hill, 1974.